THE BOOK OF TRAINS

First published in Great Britain in 1968
by Macdonald and Co. (Publishers) Ltd.
Gulf House, 2 Portman Street, London,
W.1.

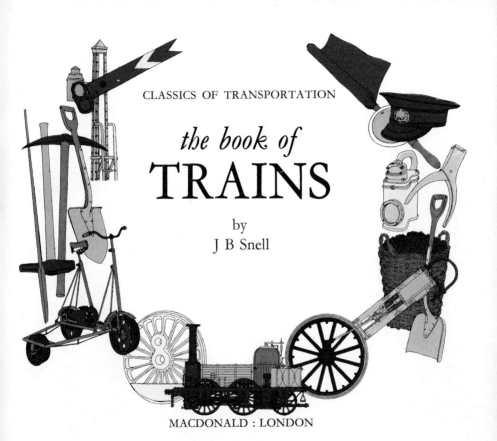

CLASSICS OF TRANSPORTATION

the book of
TRAINS

by
J B Snell

MACDONALD : LONDON

We tend to think of the steam engine as a relatively modern concept; actually an awareness of the power to be derived from steam dates back to classical times. Had the technology of the Greeks or Romans been as well developed as their science, and had they possessed an abundant source of fuel, the Industrial Revolution might have come about two thousand years earlier than it did. But as it happened, the first practical use of the power of steam was during the seventeenth century, when it was applied to the task of pumping water out of coalmines in Britain; a nice illustration of the way in which one step forward in industrial development springs out of, and depends on, an earlier one. For the coalmines were there first, to meet the need for fuel that Britain's denuded forests could no longer supply, and the voracious appetite of the first primitive engines for coal could hardly be satisfied anywhere far from a pithead. Carts running on the battered ruins of the old Roman roads, and packhorses elsewhere, could carry all that mediaeval society required, but better transport was needed to support industrialization. One possible answer was to develop inland waterways by deepening rivers or building entirely new canals, and much was done in

The interior of a roundhouse on the Pennsylvania Railroad in the 1880s.

this way during and after the seventeenth century. But waterways were impractical in hilly places. Roadbuilding was not much easier, since enormous quantities of stone were needed, especially in those level and usually prosperous districts furthest from quarries where roads were most wanted. Very often a better proposition was the railway, on which wheeled vehicles were pulled along on tracks. This had appeared during the sixteenth century; by the end of the eighteenth it was very common in mining areas, and beginning to be used elsewhere.

But land transport still depended entirely on animal power, as it had always done. The first steam engines, working not strictly by steam pressure but by atmospheric pressure against the vacuum left when steam condensed, were far too heavy and cumbersome to move. It was not until the much lighter and more economical "high-pressure" engine, which substituted the pressure of expanding steam for condensation and vacuum, began to be used at the end of the eighteenth century that the use of the new power in transport became possible. Several men built steam engines for use on roads, but met with trouble; the machines were too heavy, damaged the surface, frightened horses, and were a menace to other travellers. The time was not yet ripe for the powered road vehicle. It was on the railway, where a highly-developed private track was available, that the steam locomotive found its destiny as the creation of man which has done more to change the face of the world than any other. Thus February 13th, 1804, when Richard Trevithick drove the first locomotive over the $9\frac{1}{2}$ miles of the Penydarran Railway, near Merthyr in South Wales, hauling a train loaded with iron, marked the beginning of a new age.

Early days on the Black Forest Railway.

HOW A STEAM LOCOMOTIVE WORKS —THE BOILER

The obvious place to start an account of how a steam locomotive works is the boiler, where the steam is produced. Its function is to raise as much steam as is required as cheaply as possible—that is, for the lowest practical cost in fuel, construction, and maintenance. To save fuel it is necessary to extract the greatest possible proportion of heat from its burning. Most early locomotive builders used a boiler rather like those then used to power stationary engines; a barrel part-full of water containing one large inner tube, which held the fire. Coal was fed in at one end of this tube, and smoke and hot gases came out the other. Since the tube was wide and relatively short, this arrangement was exceedingly wasteful, with a large volume in relation to its surface; most of the heat never got near the water and was lost, merely causing the chimney to glow red-hot. However, this was the normal boiler at first, even though Trevithick himself had gone one better by making the tube U-shaped, which greatly increased the heating surface and reduced coal consumption. But it was clear that a still further improvement would be obtained by using many small tubes instead of one large one. After much

experiment, two engineers, Robert Stephenson in Newcastle and Marc Seguin near Lyons, simultaneously produced types of multi-tubular boilers in 1829; and it was from Stephenson's design, as modified in 1830, that conventional modern locomotive boilers descend.

The main body of a boiler is called the barrel; at one end this contains the firebox, which is surrounded by water. A large number of small tubes (usually over 100) connect the firebox through the barrel with the smokebox and chimney. All hot gases produced by the fire must pass through these tubes. The details of design may vary considerably in matters of proportion, for instance to give a larger grate area to suit low-grade fuel, or to improve the whole thing considered as an engineering structure. The boiler barrel is composed of steel plates (originally wrought-iron) riveted together, or in the most modern practice welded. The wooden planking often seen in pictures of early engines was heat insulation; it has long been replaced by plaster or asbestos lagging, in turn concealed by thin steel sheeting which forms the outer cover of the boiler. Fireboxes were originally usually made of copper, chosen because it is a good conductor of heat, but now they are normally of steel, which is stronger and cheaper. Similarly, brass tubes have been replaced by steel ones.

Early boilers produced steam at a pressure of 25 to 50 pounds per square inch; modern ones anywhere from 200 to 300 pounds. The gradual move towards higher pressures was for two reasons; firstly, to obtain more power within the limits of space and weight, a factor more urgent to the design of locomotives than stationary or marine engines; and secondly, to increase efficiency. It takes a lot of fuel to turn water into steam in the first place, but only a little more to develop steam at a higher pressure, at which it can do proportionately more work. However, there was an upward limit to this process because it proved difficult to build and maintain conventional locomotive boilers working at more than 280—300 pounds pressure, and experiment failed to adapt the different types of boiler used in stationary power plants, capable of producing steam at several thousand pounds pressure, to locomotive conditions.

On the other hand, it was also found around the turn of the century that in practice the amount of work to be derived from a given quantity and pressure of steam could be increased by making it hotter, and here was another considerable improvement in efficiency. Thereafter, superheaters were normally added. These consist of long, thin, U-shaped tubes conveying steam on its way to the cylinders, placed inside certain ordinary boiler tubes (made larger for the purpose) directly heated by hot gases from the fire.

CYLINDERS AND FRONT ENDS

The cylinders are the muscles of a steam engine: here, pushing against a piston, steam produces power. The complication lies in getting steam into and out of each end of each cylinder at the right moment. In the earliest days, steam was admitted to the cylinder through almost the whole length of the piston's stroke, but it was soon realized that this was wasteful; even having doubled its volume, the steam was still capable of doing more work. So "expansive working" was introduced, where the driver was able to vary the length of stroke during which steam was admitted, and bring the "cut-off" point down to below 50%. With superheating, it became possible to work satisfactorily with cut-off as early as 15% or even less, with considerable economy. An alternative way of allowing the steam to expand to the same extent was to use it in two cylinders successively, first a small high-pressure and then a large low-pressure one; this was known as compound working. In practice, compound locomotives were usually able to achieve a fuel saving of around 10% compared with an equivalent simple locomotive, but at the expense of additional cylinders and valve gear so that it became a matter of opinion whether the process was financially worthwhile. Compounding was tried in most countries, and was very popular for a while until superheating came in; afterwards, most railways lost interest, and it was really only the French who continued to use compounds on a large scale and to demonstrate that the economy of compounding could be added to that of superheating.

Steam admission and exhaust to and from the cylinders is controlled by valves, of which two types have been most widely used. The first, the slide or flat valve, came in at the beginning; it consisted of a casting shaped rather like a flat U or open D, which moved to and fro across a flat surface containing two openings or "ports" connecting with each end of the cylinder, and, in the centre, another leading to the chimney. At the end of its stroke the valve uncovered one port outside one arm of the "D", allowing steam to enter one end of the cylinder, while the other port was then open to the inner side of the "D", allowing steam from that end of the cylinder to escape to exhaust. Simple enough, but with one drawback: the valve was forced down hard onto its flat working surface by steam at high pressure; this caused considerable friction and so driving the valve consumed a lot of power. This disadvantage was overcome by the piston valve, which evolved out of the slide valve around the turn of the century; in principle it was exactly the same, but the flat working surface became the inside of a cylinder and the valve a double piston, dumb-bell shaped. Since it was not forced hard against the ports, friction and loss of power were reduced to a negligible amount; eventually (but not generally until the 1920s) it was realized that this meant that there was no longer any objection to making the valve as large, and increasing the length of its travel as much, as was necessary to avoid any throttling of steam as it passed through the ports; and so an important cause of loss of power and hindrance to fast running was removed.

Either kind of valve is driven by valve gear, which relates its motion to that of the piston and driving wheels and so ensures that steam is admitted and exhausted at the right moment. Types of valve gear are legion, but two predominate: in nineteenth-century practice, that devised by Robert Stephenson in the 1830s; and in twentieth-century practice, that devised by Eugene Walschaerts in 1844.

Having passed through the cylinders the steam is exhausted through the blastpipe and up the chimney, where it has one final function, in inducing a draught through the tubes and so through the fire. The beauty of this is that it is a simple feed-back arrangement; the harder the locomotive is worked, the fiercer the blast of the exhaust, and so the greater the draught and the hotter the fire. However, with the single blastpipe and chimney normally used, there is a considerable power loss here, which is evidenced by the impressive noise most steam locomotives make when putting out a large effort. The reason for this waste of energy is that the exhaust steam comes out of the blastpipe so fast it punches its way through the smokebox gases rather than achieving its greatest effect in propelling them out of the chimney, and therefore it is a rather inefficient draught-inducer. The way round this is to reduce the pressure of the exhaust steam (by making it expand further and do more work in the cylinders) and to enlarge the blastpipe area, while at the same time increasing the effect on the smokebox gases by having two or more blastpipe nozzles and a correspondingly enlarged chimney. These developments only began during the second quarter of the twentieth century, and various multiple-jet blastpipe arrangements, connected with the names of Chapelon, Kylala, and Lemaitre among others, came into fairly general use. But since improvements in this area involved research into the unknown field of the behaviour of gas flows at high speeds, not otherwise explored except by designers of rockets and supersonic aircraft, many practical railwaymen soon lost patience and went back to good old unscientific rule-of-thumb practice. The Giesl Ejector, the most effective multiple-jet blastpipe arrangement, using seven nozzles in line combined with an oblong chimney, was not perfected until after 1950; it came too late to be applied to steam locomotives in most countries. It gave a fuel saving of around 10% plus increased power, but it had already been decided to change over to diesels (for the sake of a fuel saving of around 10% plus increased power).

The viaduct carrying the Gotthard main line over the Maderaner gorge at Amsteg, in Switzerland, in 1883.

WHEELS AND WHEEL ARRANGEMENTS

In the early days it was believed that in order to reach high speeds it was necessary for a locomotive to have large driving wheels, since no piston could move at more than a certain number of strokes per minute. So there were engines with very large wheels indeed; a diameter of eight feet was not uncommon in the mid-nineteenth century for main line passenger work where fast running was called for, and nine and even ten-foot wheels were also used. But it was rare for any of these machines to touch speeds over eighty miles an hour, and generally top speeds were not much above sixty. The limiting factor was really the design of valves and cylinders; after these had been improved in the way already outlined, and especially after the general adoption of large piston valves in the 1920s, very much higher speeds became possible. Engines with driving wheels little over six feet in diameter were capable of exceeding a hundred miles an hour, and proportionate speeds could be reached with smaller wheels. Small driving wheels remained useful for locomotives designed for pull rather than pace, as in mountain or freight work, but there was a general rule of

thumb that the very smallest wheel practical for main-line work was the same diameter as the track gauge. Beyond this point general wear and tear became too heavy.

There was another factor which limited maximum speed: balancing. Masses of metal in the form of pistons, connecting rods, and coupling rods flying round and round or to and fro develop rhythmically irregular forces which have a more disturbing effect as speed increases, eventually becoming capable of lifting wheels right off the track. Revolving weights, like coupling rods, can be cancelled out easily enough by balance weights on the other side of the wheels, but reciprocating weights, like pistons and connecting rods, are more difficult and can only be imperfectly balanced by revolving balance weights. This puts a limitation on speed independent of anything that happens to the steam in the cylinders, and it became a powerful argument in favour of using more than two cylinders for high-speed locomotives, since with three and especially with four it became possible to arrange for the reciprocating parts largely to balance themselves.

Wheel arrangements, on the other hand, were subject to a different set of principles. The number of driving wheels was the first thing that had to be decided; one used as few as possible on general grounds of expense, but on the other hand the amount of low-speed pull, or tractive effort, a locomotive could apply effectively without the wheels slipping on the rail depended strictly on the total weight, or adhesive weight, as it was known, which the driving wheels carried. And the maximum weight that can be carried on any one axle is always a known limit, depending on the strength of track and bridges. Hence, although single driving wheels were common at first, as train weights increased they began to be replaced by multiple drivers, first in freight and later in passenger service, and by the twentieth century they had almost vanished. Correspondingly, the average number of wheels coupled together tended to increase as time went on, although locomotives with more than ten wheels coupled were never common. Generally, if more tractive effort than this was needed, it became necessary to use one or another variety of articulated locomotive, with two (or more) sets of cylinders and wheels mounted independently in order to accommodate themselves to curves. It was soon found advantageous to provide one or two carrying wheels with a controlled amount of sideplay at the front of the locomotive; the main reason was to improve smooth running at speed, and to guide the machine gently into curves, but another reason was to allow more room for larger cylinders. Carrying wheels at the rear end of the locomotive were provided for a different reason; rare at first (except on tank engines) they became necessary as locomotives grew bigger, and therefore required larger boilers and fireboxes. It then often became difficult to find room for a firebox above the driving wheels, so it had to be placed behind them, where one or two (or sometimes even three) pairs of wheels were needed to carry its weight. This meant that a lower proportion of the engine's total weight was available for adhesion, but this drawback had to be faced. Fortunately great adhesive weight was most important at low speeds, and engines designed for low-speed work seldom needed large fireboxes.

So the selection of the appropriate wheel arrangement for a new locomotive depended on the kind of work it was going to do, and a nice judgement of all these factors.

THE STEAM LOCOMOTIVE IN TRAFFIC

One reason why many people have criticized steam locomotives is because they are dirty. To a large extent this is because most of them burn coal, which is a dirty fuel, and as other fuels have become available men have become less tolerant of the grime they once thought unavoidable. "Where there's muck there's brass" is an unpopular motto nowadays.

But steam locomotives are not as dirty as all that; it all depends on how often they are cleaned. It is interesting to observe how those railways which said that the replacement of their dirty steamers by nice clean diesels would enable them to smarten up and improve their public image, tend now to be running dirty diesels.

Apart from this one sore point, the steam engine is a docile and uncomplicated creature. It does demand watering facilities at strategic points, which can be embarrassing in dry countries, and fuelling and ash-removal plant, but otherwise its needs are modest and can be met with simple equipment. Unlike those who deal with internal combustion engines, the steam man doesn't have to think in terms of thousandths of an inch. Of course, care, precision, and intelligence do pay; but

Mantaua Junction, West Philadelphia, showing a system of interlacing tracks.

they are not essential. A steamer will keep on slogging away in the face of neglect that would completely stop any other power.

Why, then, are these congenial beasts being slaughtered? This is not quite as easy a question to answer as we are sometimes told. The electric locomotive, where electrification is practicable, is superior on all counts to both steam and diesel; but on non-electrified track the question is more interesting. We hear about increased availability, and how a diesel can do more work than a steamer per 24 hours, but this is only part of the truth. When like has been compared with like, and a really modern steam engine compared with a diesel which is its contemporary in design (which hasn't often happened), the honours have been pretty equal, especially considering steam's advantage in having a lower first cost. But generally speaking, there are three factors which have told against steam, apart from the comparative rarity of up-to-date types in most countries.

Firstly, in most places coal has tended to rise in price, while oil has become relatively cheaper. Since fuel costs are important, this has been a major reason for the changeover. Steam engines can of course burn oil also, but not as efficiently as diesels.

Secondly, although plenty remained to be done in detail, as regards brute power output steam was approaching a practical limit in most countries, and had arguably begun to go beyond it in the U.S. Engines with 30-ton axleloads made great demands on the permanent way, while in some cases the draughts needed to maintain steam in enormous boilers caused actual damage to fireboxes and tubes through cindercutting, which was a serious nuisance. And although there were steam locomotives of 10,000 horsepower, much more than double the power of any diesel so far, still there was no limit to the number of diesels that could be worked together by one crew through multiple-unit controls.

Finally, steam's very simplicity began to count against it in a changing world. In general, it needed unskilled labour; the diesel needed a somewhat smaller number of more highly skilled men. With a higher standard of living and the spread of education, the unskilled man has become more expensive, while the technician, partly because he is more numerous and partly because he still insists on wearing a clean collar, can no longer command his old premium on the labour market. (This is also the reason why coal has become expensive; mining is dirty work). So what once seemed to be steam's strongest point has, in the advanced countries, turned into its most decisive disadvantage.

And so the development of reciprocating steam locomotives has come to an end. They helped to change the world, and that change was fatal to them. Tens of thousands are still running, and in places they will probably see out the twentieth century; but the vital spark of faith in them, and in their continued improvement, has gone out. I hope the following collection of drawings and descriptions will invoke the days when it still glowed.

*Locomotives from the early beginnings in
the nineteenth century to the streamlined
ones of present days are shown on the
following pages in full-colour drawings.*

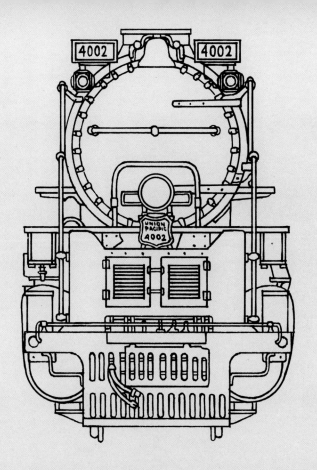

PENYDARRAN RAILWAY: TREVITHICK'S LOCOMOTIVE (1804)

The world's first railway locomotive, which ran on the Penydarran Railway in February 1804, was not long-lived; it broke the cast-iron rails too frequently and was soon taken out of service and converted to a stationary engine. No contemporary drawings or pictures of it have survived; this is in fact Trevithick's second locomotive, built at Gateshead in 1805, but believed to be closely similar. One cylinder, mounted inside the boiler barrel, drove a large flywheel which in turn drove the wheels through gearing. The engine worked flywheel leading: its operator stood on a flat truck hauled behind, endeavouring to avoid execution by the crosshead whirling in and out like a trombone-slide, and feeding in coal through the firedoor below the cylinder. Trevithick used the U-tube boiler, more expensive but much more efficient than its successors, so the chimney was at the same end as the firebox. The handle above the crosshead slide was connected to the valve (driven by a lug on the piston-rod) and used for reversing.

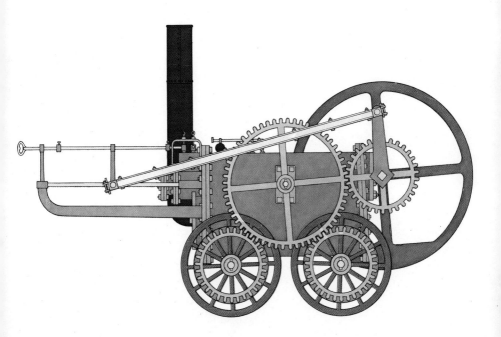

MIDDLETON RAILWAY:
BLENKINSOP'S ENGINE (1812)

Four locomotives were built to this pattern by Matthew Murray of Leeds to the order of John Blenkinsop, and worked on the 3½-mile Middleton Railway nearby for some thirty years. They were the first commercially successful locomotives in the world, but though they look less primitive, they were not in fact as advanced as Trevithick's machine of eight years earlier. Although Trevithick had demonstrated the contrary, Blenkinsop (and others) still believed the friction between iron wheel and iron rail was not enough to allow an engine to haul a useful load, so these were powered through a gear wheel engaging in lugs cast onto the outside edges of the rail. The use of two cylinders enabled the cumbersome flywheel to be abolished, but this was the only step forward; the boiler had the wasteful single straight flue, while used steam escaped through a separate silencer and exhaust pipe. The fire therefore had no forced draught, so the engines usually had to stop for a "blow-up" to restore pressure en route. They were certainly cheaper than horses, but only because the Napoleonic Wars had forced up the price of grain and feedstuffs.

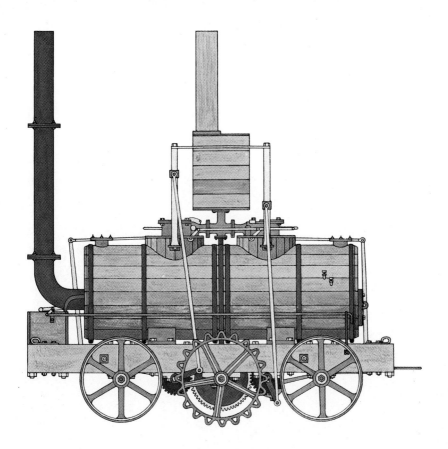

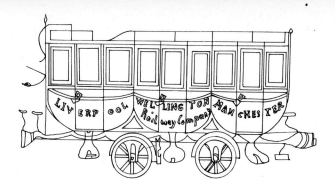

LIVERPOOL & MANCHESTER RAILWAY: STEPHENSON'S "ROCKET"

Quite the most famous of all early locomotives, the "Rocket" was built by Robert Stephenson as his firm's entry for the Liverpool & Manchester Railway's Rainhill Trials in 1829. It followed fifteen years of development since Blenkinsop, but was itself a giant step forward. Cylinders had been placed outside the boiler for some time, but only lately had they been removed from the vertical and coupled directly to the wheels; the decisive improvement in the "Rocket" was due to the introduction of boiler tubes, in combination with every other feature of best contemporary practice. The "Rocket" won the competition fairly easily, being the only of the three entrants to haul the required fifteen tons for sixty miles at ten miles an hour without breakdown; indeed, she proved capable of over 30 m.p.h. But she was all the same very much a prototype; the following year Stephenson adopted a firebox mounted inside the boiler in place of the external waterjacketed version.

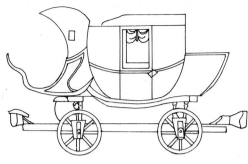

LIVERPOOL & MANCHESTER RAILWAY: 0-4-2 "LION" (1838)

This engine was built by Todd, Kitson & Laird for the Liverpool & Manchester Railway in 1838, by which time little 5-ton 4-wheelers like the "Rocket" had been outclassed and overwhelmed by the weight of traffic. For its date it was a conventional machine of very respectable size, with the then advanced feature of "sandwich" frames, in which the wheels ran between parallel frame-plates with bearings on either side, four per axle. This meant that derailment would not inevitably follow axle breakage, at that time an event frequent enough to be a serious danger. "Lion" served the L & M and later the London & North Western for some thirty years before it was retired and converted into a stationary pumping engine. Half a century later, as it was about to be finally scrapped, its value was realized and instead it was rebuilt. Now the property of a railway enthusiasts' society, it is still working and runs from time to time, often to star in films.

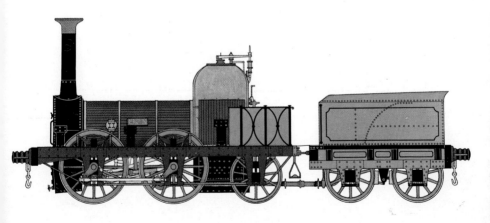

31

BALTIMORE & OHIO RAILROAD: 4-2-0 "LAFAYETTE" (1837)

This machine is interesting in that it marks the point where American locomotive development began to follow a separate course. The earliest American engines had been imported from Britain; the first distinctive transatlantic design, Phineas Davis's vertical-boilered four-wheelers, proved to be a blind alley, although a long-lived one, for vertical boilers could only be built up to a certain quite modest size. The most important difference between European and American railways during the early years was that the Americans had neither time nor money to spend in obtaining a level and perfect permanent way, and locomotives with rigid wheel-bases frequently derailed as a result. But an independently-mounted set of wheels in front could, it was found, follow the irregularities of the rails much more accurately; hence the bogie, as here. The "Lafayette", built in Philadelphia in 1837, was the Baltimore & Ohio's first engine with horizontal boiler and more than four wheels; it marked an important step forward, and is still preserved in working order by the company.

33

BALTIMORE & OHIO RAILROAD: "CAMELBACK" 0-8-0 no. 65 (1848)

Not all American locomotives had bogies by any means; hauling freight over mountains, speed was low and derailment unlikely, while the greatest possible adhesive weight was vital. During the 1840s engines with eight coupled wheels began to be used, so this machine was not particularly unusual on that count; but it is also an early example of a purely American oddity, which in some cases lasted until the end of steam, the "Camelback". This consisted of a separate cab on top of the boiler for the driver; the fireman stayed in his original position. The advantage of this was that the driver had a better view forward, which became more important on later engines with bigger boilers and fireboxes difficult to see round; and this explains why the "Camelback", although always rare, managed to survive over a century. Here the driver has a positive pavilion all to himself, and the fireman a mere awning; later the proportions of the two cabs were reversed, with the driver packed neatly in between boiler and the undersides of overbridges.

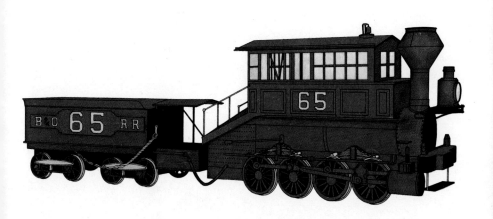

NORTHERN RAILWAY OF FRANCE: CRAMPTON 4-2-0 (1859)

Designers of early express locomotives had a dual problem: how to combine a large driving wheel with a low centre of gravity, considered necessary for safety. This was difficult because a high axle was incompatible with a low boiler, although one engine at least was built with a suitable hole in the boiler. The neatest reconciliation was that of T. R. Crampton, who placed the driving wheels behind the boiler; although this meant it was difficult to get much weight on them, it helped with speed. Crampton was English, but his engines were regarded as freaks in Britain and the USA, and did best in France. This particular one, built by Cail of Lille in 1859, was the last of 58 for the Nord; it had driving wheels only 6' 10" in diameter, by no means large for a machine of this type. The SNCF still owns a working Crampton used for special occasions.

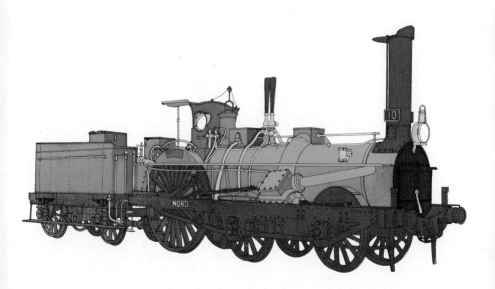

37

THE "AMERICAN TYPE" 4-4-0
(c. 1860)

This pattern is certainly one of the locomotive classics; the type was a mainstay of railroading in the American style for half a century. It first developed in the 1840s, evolving very naturally out of the "Lafayette" design as soon as the tractive effort of a single pair of driving wheels became insufficient. This particular example was built in 1860, by which time the species was mature. A few early variants had inside cylinders, but normally these were outside. Cowcatchers, vast oil headlamps, and diamond-shaped spark-arresting chimneys have all passed into legend, but plenty of engines always burnt coal instead of wood and had "straight-shooter" chimneys. By the 1890s engines of this pattern had been outclassed and were slowly disappearing. Modernized 4-4-0s did have a brief run as economical lightweight passenger engines after 1920, but now they have gone and throughout the world only a few are left more or less as museum pieces.

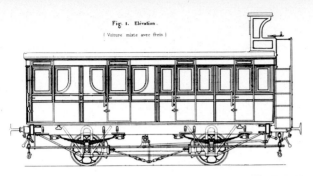

Fig. 1. Élévation.

(Voiture mixte avec frein)

WESTERN RAILWAY OF FRANCE: 774 SERIES 2-4-0 (1870)

While the 4-4-0 was the universal locomotive in America, the 2-4-0 enjoyed a long popularity for passenger work in Europe. Better permanent way meant that the leading bogie could be dispensed with in favour of a simpler rigid single front carrying axle, while a boiler capable of delivering the required power could still be accommodated on the shorter frame. European custom was also slower to accept an adequate cab for the crew. So far, this particular engine, one of a series of 154 built for the Ouest between 1863 and 1875, is reasonably typical, but in other respects it is rather unusual, notably in the combination of outside valves (driven by Stephenson gear) with inside cylinders, and conspicuous exhaust steampipes.

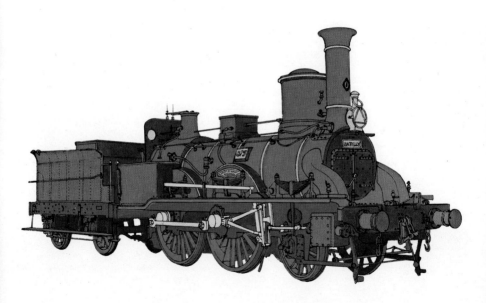

SPANISH NATIONAL RAILWAYS: 2031 CLASS 0-8-0 (1864)

The use of eight-coupled locomotives on main-line freight work, especially in mountain districts, was common in Europe quite as early as it was in America. This one was built in France for a constituent of the Madrid—Zaragoza—Allicante Railway in 1864; apart from running on 5' 6" gauge tracks it was like hundreds working in France, Italy, and elsewhere, and a thoroughly modern and practical heavy-duty design of its period. There cannot have been much wrong with it, as it was one of several still in service over a hundred years later, and very little changed. The original plain weatherboard has been replaced by (or perhaps incorporated in) a cab, and vacuum and steam brakes have been added, but the rest still remains as evidence of a remarkably good original investment.

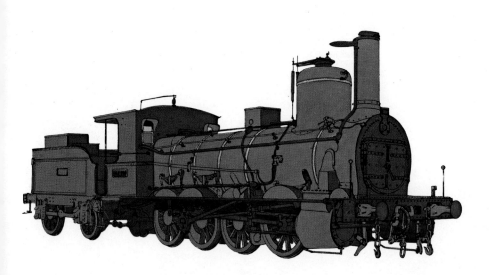

43

NEW YORK & HARLEM RAILROAD: FORNEY 0-4-4-T (c. 1870)

Tank engines have always been quite rare in North America, which was an odd thing. Vast though the continent may be, there were plenty of short-distance jobs, especially suburban passenger runs, where a handily bi-directional tank engine would have been useful. But few lines used them; the majority preferred to keep on laboriously turning tender engines (and indeed kept on doing so in most cases when diesels came). M. N. Forney patented this design of eight-wheeled tank engine in 1866; basically it can be regarded as an 0-4-0 tender engine on a continuous rigid frame which also carried the tender, supported at the rear end by a bogie. Coal and water were both carried in the tender portion, deferring to the standard American criticism of tank engines that their adhesive weight dwindled as the water was used. But its long wheelbase made a Forney better suited to fast running than an 0-4-0. Later, larger successors to this engine worked the New York Elevated until electrification around 1900.

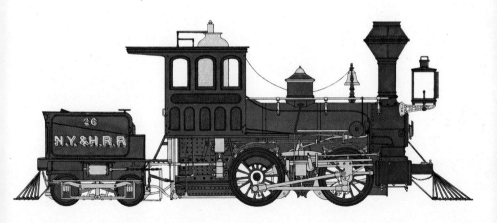

BELGIAN NATIONAL RAILWAYS: 51 CLASS 0-6-0T (c. 1885)

The Belgian 51 class tanks were built from 1866 to 1904: quite a long run for the same design, even with minor alterations from time to time. All of them had the rather unusual "pannier" tanks, mounted high alongside the boiler and allowing access to the machinery for inspection and oiling, but without causing quite such a high centre of gravity as a saddle tank which went right over the top of the boiler. The square chimney became a Belgian trade-mark for a period, and was fitted to a wide range of engines; it is difficult to see its technical justification, and it needs the trained eye of the design consultant to see beauty in it, but it certainly makes an impact. The cab was unusual in being open at the front as well as the back and sides: it must have offered little shelter from the winter gales at Ostend.

47

PRUSSIAN STATE RAILWAYS: 0-4-2T NO. 1577 (1882)

This locomotive was one of a large number of small tank engines with varying details belonging to the Prussian State Railways, and is perhaps a better example of the mainstream of European design of machines of this nature than the Belgian pannier tank on the previous page. It was built at Hanover in 1882, and spent its entire working life of some forty years on local duties around Berlin. From its relatively large driving wheels it was clearly intended for passenger work; similar 0-6-2Ts of this size but with inside cylinders worked in Britain until the mid 1960s.

FRENCH STATE RAILWAYS: STEAM RAILCAR NO. 1 (1879)

The branch line problem is nothing new: how to devise some economical vehicle to convey small numbers of passengers, instead of an ordinary train which is essentially a mass-producer of transport, was a problem that vexed railway engineers at an early date. The first steam rail-car ran on the broad-gauge Tiverton branch of the Great Western in 1847, and an 84-seater was built in 1848 for the Angel Road-Enfield branch of the Eastern Counties Railway, near London. But they never became common. This automotrice à vapeur, *dating from much later, is unusual in combining a locomotive portion with one of the then fairly common double-deck coaches, to give a really multi-purpose vehicle with first, second, and third class, mail, and baggage accommodation. The driver cannot have had a very good view when running in reverse, so perhaps the equipage was turned.*

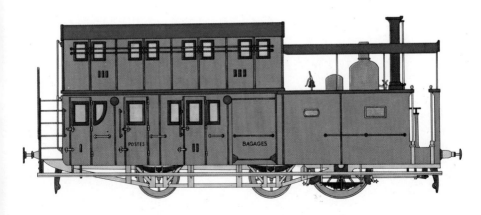

POSTES   BAGAGES

51

MIDLAND RAILWAY: JOHNSON
4-2-2 (1887)

*By the late 1870s train weights in Britain,
as they had earlier elsewhere, began to
pass beyond the limits of what could
comfortably be handled by an engine with
one pair of driving wheels. But the invention
of the steam sander, which delivered a
more or less reliable flow of sand under
the driving wheel when required, gave a
new lease of life to the single, and together
with an axleloading of over 20 tons brought
it back for a while into the field of practical
possibility. These machines, designed by S. W.
Johnson for the Midland Railway, were the
most powerful British singles, and the last;
a few survived into the 1920s. Admittedly the
Midland made a fetish of small engines, with
a great deal of double-heading of expresses,
and even so found it necessary to standardize on
4-4-0s shortly after; but the Johnson 4-2-2s
were an excellent engineering job and long
continued on lighter trains. The steam sanding
pipes can be seen in the drawing.*

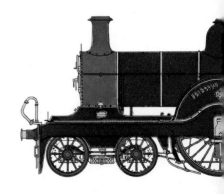

PARIS-LYONS-MEDITERRANEAN RAILWAY: CLASS C 4-4-0 (1894)

This locomotive was one of a series which worked the principal expresses on the PLM main line from Paris to Marseilles and the Riviera around the turn of the century. The first 20 class Cs were 4-cylinder compound 4-4-0s built in 1892; the next batch of 40 (including this one) had this early form of streamlining (they were officially called "windcutters"), while the final 120, built from 1895 to 1902, were rather larger but similarly streamlined. The Cs were successful enough, but could not have owed very much to their windcutting capabilities; at the time the speed limit was 75 m.p.h. Several of the final series survived to become class 230A after nationalisation in 1938. The V-shaped cab became a PLM trade-mark, and is still to be seen on the 241P class 4-8-2s of 1947, among other engines in France and elsewhere.

GREAT NORTHERN RAILWAY:
4-4-2 NO. 990 (1898)

One interesting piece of continuity in British locomotive practice has been the long-established policy of using more powerful locomotives on the level East Coast main line than on the much more difficult Midland or West Coast routes. This has even persisted under dieselization, but it was followed throughout the great years of steam, and can be traced back at least as far as 1898, when H. A. Ivatt designed these, the first British Atlantics. They were a step forward in power, but were soon outclassed by the more famous and successful large-boilered and wide-fireboxed version which appeared four years later. Both classes originally used saturated steam, and were fitted with superheaters some ten years later. The large-boilered Atlantics survived the second world war, and some very similar ones built for the London, Brighton and South Coast worked until 1958, proving the basic mechanical soundness of Ivatt's original design. Indeed, no other British 4-2-2 proved as successful. No. 990, together with the long-boilered no. 251, still exist in operable condition.

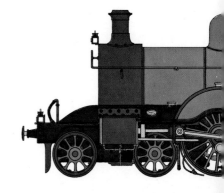

BALTIMORE & OHIO RAILROAD: A9 CLASS 4-4-2 (1904)

The 4-4-2 locomotive, primarily intended for fast passenger service, was first widely used in America during the 1890s: the type got the name "Atlantic" through the exploits of the flyers between Philadelphia and Atlantic City in 1896. It had a fairly brief run in the USA, since train weights soon increased beyond the capacity of four driving wheels: but since it allowed ample space for a large firebox the Atlantic layout was well suited for fast lightweight trains and was in fact revived in stream-lined form during the 1930s. This B & O engine of 1904 is a good example of how the type had evolved towards the end of its first incarnation; an only moderately large firebox and driving wheels on this one show that it was intended more for local passenger work (over long distances) than dramatic sprints. In 1904 the Americans were still addicted to inside valve gear, and the inwards slope of the massive combined cylinder and valve and smokebox saddle castings allowed the piston valves to be driven directly by this.

NEW ZEALAND RAILWAYS:
Q CLASS 4-6-2 (1901)

These 3' 6" gauge engines are usually considered to be the first class of "Pacifics" in the world, although there had been earlier individual locomotives with that wheel arrangement. They were built by the Baldwin Locomotive works of Philadelphia in 1901. The design originated because the NZR wanted an express locomotive with a large grate, suitable for burning the lignite coal mined south of Dunedin, and the idea of a camelback 4-6-0 had to be rejected because of loading gauge restrictions. Instead, a normal cab and a carrying wheel to bear the lengthened rear end was decided on. So first appeared what was to become the twentieth century's most popular and versatile type, numerous in nearly every country (Russia was the main exception), whose wheel arrangement gave good riding at speed and also room for the largest boiler and cylinders that could usefully drive six coupled wheels in general main line work. Why it was called a "Pacific" is arguable: perhaps because it was bigger than an "Atlantic". The "Q" class survived until 1956.

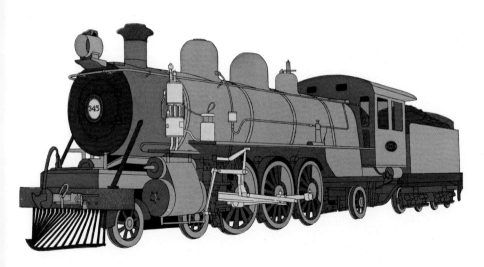

PRUSSIAN STATE RAILWAYS: P8
CLASS 4-6-0 (1906)

These were the last and largest but one of the Prussian State Railways' 4-6-0s, and became a standard German type: nearly four thousand were built between 1906 and 1924. Their early success was partly due to the fact that they were some of the first locomotives to be fitted with super-heaters. An excellent straight-forward two-cylinder mixed-traffic design with no frills, they were a reliable, cheap, and popular "jack-of-all-trades"; they also packed a useful amount of power onto a sixteen-ton axle-loading which allowed them to run nearly everywhere. Whether as war reparations or as engines built new to foreign order, fleets of them were owned by most countries between Belgium and Russia (inclusive). After sixty years their ranks are thinning in Germany, but in Eastern Europe they are still numerous.

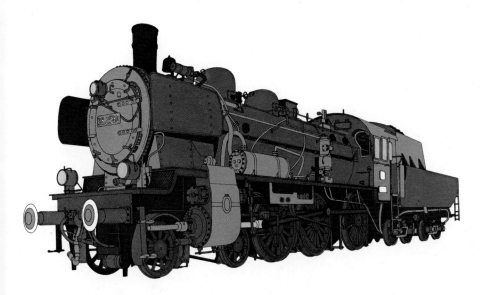

EASTERN RAILWAY OF FRANCE: 11 CLASS 4-6-0 (1903)

The first two express passenger 4-6-0s of the Est company were built at their Epernay works in 1903; following extended trials, main production of the class started in 1906 and by 1925 a total of 180 were in service. They were four-cylinder compounds, with 6' 10" wheels; superheating, together with other front-end improvements after 1930 enabled them to hold their own on high-speed work with loads of up to 350 tons against Pacifics and even 4-8-2s. After 1938 they were classified 230K. In 1948 twelve were streamlined to work a new flyer from Paris to Strasbourg, a duty they performed for nearly a decade. The last survivor was retired in 1965.

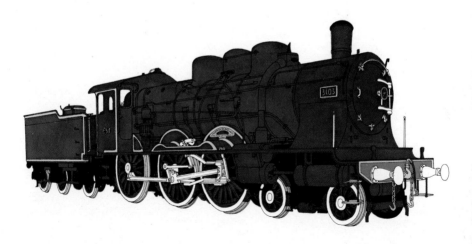

SWEDISH STATE RAILWAYS:
E2 CLASS 2-8-0 (1908)

The Swedes were unusually fond of inside-cylinder engines, and had a very large proportion of them. The drawback of the inside-cylinder arrangement was the difficulty of access to the machinery for lubrication and maintenance, the need to employ an expensive crank axle, and some limit to maximum cylinder size. The advantages, however, were smoother riding, due to the reciprocating parts being nearer to the centre line of the engine, and reduction in weight because one casting for both inside cylinders weighed less than two separate ones for outside cylinders. Under Swedish conditions, which included a lot of track with restricted axle loadings, these were considered decisive. The inside-cylinder 2-8-0 is a very rare type, but quite common in Sweden, and although the Swedish railways are nominally all diesel or electric, the considerable number of steam engines retained in the operating reserve includes many of them.

ADRIATIC RAILWAY (ITALY)— 670 CLASS 4-6-0 (1902)

The best-known "cab-forward" locomotives were those which ran on the Southern Pacific Railroad in the United States, a series of large and powerful articulated machines which lasted until dieselization; but they were not, as often stated, quite unique. They were preceded by these Italian engines, of which 42 were built to Guiseppe Zara's design between 1902 and 1906. The point of the design, in both Italy and America, was to lessen the smoke nuisance to enginemen in tunnels; working on a steam locomotive hauling a heavy train slowly uphill in a long single-line tunnel can be a literally suffocating experience. Various expedients have been tried from time to time to combat this, including comical horizontal chimneys, but the best answer was to put the enginemen ahead of the smoke, and this was achieved by putting the cab in front. Unlike the American engines, which burnt oil which could easily be piped round the boiler from the tender, these machines were coalburners; the coal had therefore to be carried in small bunkers visible just behind the cab, and the tender contained only water (plus a brakesman's shelter).

The 670s were all four-cylinder compounds, on the Plancher system; the later ones were built with superheaters and became class 671, to which all were altered in due course. They had a fair life; the last was not taken out of service until about 1942. Some of the tenders survive to this day, conveying drinking water to outlying railwaymen's settlements.

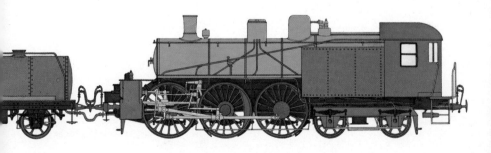

VIVARAIS RAILWAY, FRANCE:
SLM 0-6-6-0T (1903)

*Anatole Mallet's patent articulated loco-
motive had the great advantage of a long
as well as flexible wheelbase, coupled with
the possibility of using all its weight for
adhesion. So although the principle was
later taken up by main-line railways,
notably in the USA, most early Mallets were
intended for service on steep grades and
sharp curves. The true Mallet is also a
compound, with the front half using low-
pressure steam exhausted by the rear
cylinders, but many of the American ones
abandoned this practice. This example was
one of eight built in 1903 by the Schweizerische
Lokomotiv- und Maschinenfabrik of
Winterthur for the Réseau du Vivarais of
the Chemins de fer Departmentaux company.
They were the most powerful metre-
gauge locomotives in France at that time,
and had to be, as the Vivarais was an
exceedingly tough proposition with grades
as steep as 1 in 22 on its main line. One
of the eight was still working in 1966.*

71

ATCHISON, TOPEKA & SANTA FE RAILWAY: 2-10-10-2 (1911)

The Mallet type had a whirlwind period of being fashionable in the USA around 1910. Some lines experimented with the design, got to know it, and stayed faithful till the end; others, no less ardent at first, soon tired and dropped it permanently. One of the latter was the Santa Fe, which produced and disposed of a wide variety of Mallets inside ten years. This machine was a rebuild of two 2-10-2 freight engines; due to its great length it was given what was inaccurately called a "flexible boiler". In fact this consisted of a normal boiler in the rear half, linked by flexible piping and panelling to an enormous preheater occupying the front half of what appeared to be the boiler barrel, where feedwater was raised almost to boiling point by gases which had already passed through the ordinary boiler. This was the weak point of the design: intractable problems with this preheater led all ten 2-10-10-2s to be converted back to twenty ordinary locomotives in 1915.

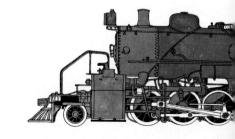

JAVANESE STATE RAILWAYS: HANNOVERSCHE 2-12-2T (1913)

The Dutch never had any particularly large locomotives working in their homeland, but their colonies made up for this; for example, with these well tanks for the 3′ 6″ gauge in Java, built by the Hannoversche Maschinenbau in 1913. Intended to supplement some older Mallets in mountain service, they weighed 74 tons and had 3′ 7¾″ driving wheels; to allow them to negotiate curves of 500 feet radius, the first and last coupled axles were free to move sideways. For descending long grades, they were fitted also with the Riggenbach counter-pressure brake, which retarded the train by compressing air in the cylinders. Large well tanks like this, in which more water was carried between the frames, were quite common in European practice. Since steam locomotives are still being delivered to Indonesia, these splendid engines are probably still working.

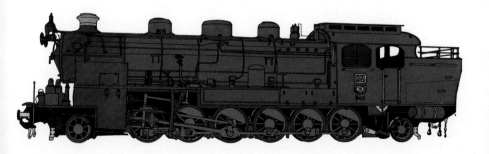

75

FRENCH NATIONAL RAILWAYS: 241A CLASS 4-8-2 (1925)

These engines, introduced by the Chemins de Fer de l'Est in 1925, were the first 4-8-2s in Europe, beating a rather similar Spanish design by a few weeks, and among the largest coalburners ever to be handfired. However, as truly French four-cylinder compounds, they were economical machines and did not make unreasonable demands on the fireman even when working their usual 18-car expresses on 60 m.p.h. bookings. (Lighter and faster trains were worked by Pacifics, or indeed the 230Ks.) Ninety had been built by 1931, half of them for the Etat (now the Western Region of the SNCF), but later they were all concentrated on the Est, and remained in charge of most of the heavy main-line passenger turns, including the Orient express out of Paris, until electrification in the early 1960s.

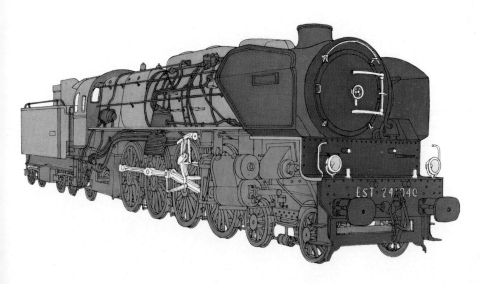

GREAT WESTERN RAILWAY: "CASTLE" CLASS 4-6-0 (1923)

In principle these modest-sized 4-6-0s date back further, since although they first appeared in 1923, their design was very closely based on the "Star" class of 1907. The fact that their four cylinders were driven by two sets of particularly inaccessible valve gear certainly dated them back to a time of cheap labour when nobody considered ease of maintenance, but they were at least thorough-breds and well engineered. Although happiest boiling along the level at some speed in the middle fifties with a not remarkably heavy train, given heroic efforts by the crew they could readily be persuaded into keeping a 70 m.p.h. overall booking, or into exceeding 100 m.p.h. downhill. But the fact that these engines, already obsolescent when they were new, were built right up to 1950, is depressing, and one can have mixed feelings also about the dramatic improvement made to them in the late 1950s by applying double chimneys and high superheat, since other railways had known about these things for years. Yet, despite all this, the heroic efforts were often made. Two "Castles" are preserved in working order.

GERMAN STATE RAILWAYS:
44 CLASS 2-10-0 (1926)

Heavy freight trains in Germany had been worked by 0-10-0s since before 1914, and so during the 1920s the next step was to introduce a heavy 2-10-0. Two types were built: the 43 class two-cylinder, and the 44 class three-cylinder. The first ten 44s were built in 1926, and were not multiplied further until 1937: but from then until 1949 over two thousand more were built, in Germany and in other countries under German occupation. However, they were rare engines compared to the lightweight 2-10-0s of classes 50 and 52, which numbered over 10,000 and 7,000 respectively. A large number of all these fine machines are still in service in several countries. The picture shows one of the original 1926 series of 44s when it was new, running without the smoke deflectors now fitted.

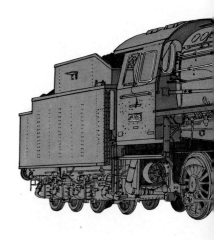

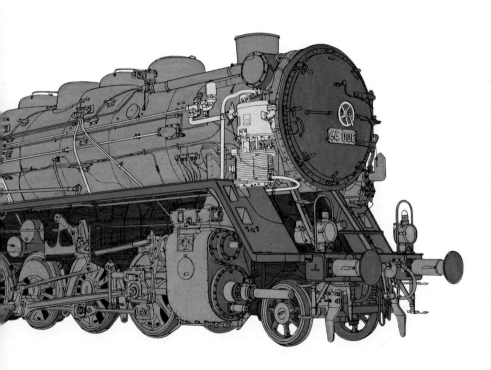

81

UNION PACIFIC RAILROAD:
9000 CLASS 4-12-2 (1926)

These were the largest non-articulated locomotives ever built, rivalled by a solitary and unsuccessful Russian 4-14-4 of 1934. They were developed from a series of 4-10-2s built by the American Locomotive Company the previous year, and like those had three cylinders; for this was the period of the brief American flirtation with three-cylinder designs and in any case it would not have been easy to find room for two cylinders large enough to make full use of the adhesion of twelve wheels, and developing nearly 97,000 lbs. of tractive effort. As in a large number of three-cylinder engines, the first driving axle had to be slightly cranked to allow the inside connecting rod, driving onto the second axle, to clear. Although primarily intended for freight haulage at speeds of up to 60 m.p.h. (with 4,000-ton loads), the 9000s were also capable of passenger work. They proved highly successful and lasted right up until dieselisation in the mid-1950s.

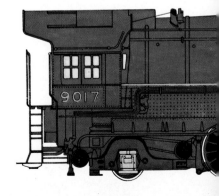

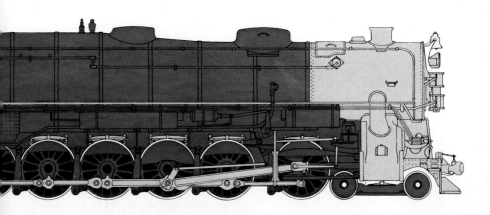

LONDON MIDLAND & SCOTTISH RAILWAY: 4F CLASS 0-6-0 (1924)

This class represents one of the unhappiest failures of imagination in locomotive history. The newly-formed LMS company found itself short of all kinds of motive power, and to fill the need for main-line freight haulage, they revamped an obsolescent Midland design and produced this to the extent of nearly six hundred machines. Certainly the LMS did a bit better later, but it was not until the second world war that the 4Fs were outnumbered by eight-coupled types. Certainly they bumbled along (although their bearings were inadequate and they suffered badly from hot boxes), and certainly they did what was required of them; the tragedy was that this was so little. Indeed, the fact that such machines were able to manage main-line freight work on Britain's largest railway as late as 1924 explains most of what was wrong with the system forty years later. The 4Fs lasted almost to the end, a gruesome memento mori of steam.

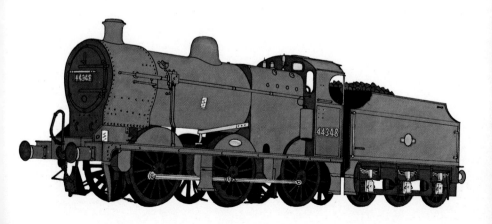

85

SOVIET RAILWAYS: JOSEPH STALIN CLASS 2-8-4 (1932)

The design of a new passenger locomotive had a low priority in post-revolutionary Russia, as one might expect. A large number of 2-6-2s of basically Tsarist design were built, but the real effort went into producing ten-coupled freight engines. However, in 1932 the first of a new class of express passenger locomotives was produced, and went into series production five years later: 650 were built before 1941. The class was named in honour of the dictator, and even after Khrushchev these engines continued to carry "J. Stalin" in cast-iron letters on their smokebox. They were a sound if unexciting design, well suited for handling the very heavy long-distance trains at the moderate speeds then ruling in Russia.

BENGAL NAGPUR RAILWAY:
de GLEHN COMPOUND 4-6-2 (1936)

India gave British engineers (and others) freedom and chance to spread themselves. In the field of locomotive design, this meant that builders had the opportunity to think big and try out ideas rejected by the conservative home market, and occasionally they made the most of the chances offered by the 5' 6" gauge and generous clearances. These 4-cylinder de Glehn compound Pacifics, built by the North British Locomotive Company, somewhat resembled the Fowler Pacifics that the LMS started to build but never finished, but were larger. Since very fast running was not required, they had rather smaller driving wheels, only 6' 3" in diameter. They were not numerous, since their heavy axleloading restricted the routes they could run on, and postwar Indian practice, as in Britain, disliked compounding.

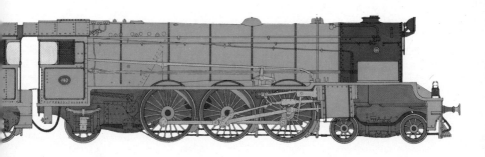

BARSI LIGHT RAILWAY:
BAGNALL 4-6-4 (1940)

The Indian railway system consists almost equally of 5' 6" and metre-gauge track, but there is also a considerable length of 2' and 2' 6" gauge in hilly or remote districts. One of the most important of these is the Barsi Light Railway, which has an impressive stud of locomotives, including the only 2' 6" gauge "Baltics" (4-6-4s) in the world. These engines were built by W. G. Bagnall, of Stafford; in working order engine and tender weigh 59 tons, and are 52 feet long overall, while their 3' 6" driving wheels combined with a modern front end enable them to maintain 50 m.p.h. quite easily, although the long rear overhang might give the crew a lively ride.

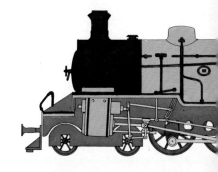

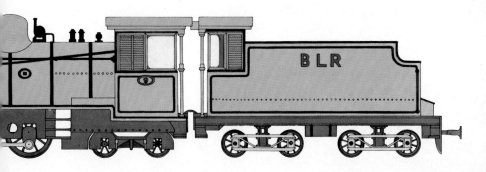

NORTHERN RAILWAYS OF FRANCE: 3.11 CLASS 4-6-2 (S.N.C.F. CLASS 231E) (1934)

These locomotives had an unusual history. They were originally built for the Paris—Orleans Railway (3501 class) between 1909 and 1914; they were worthy but unremarkable, heavy, passenger 4-cylinder compounds of that era. In 1934, a number of them were rebuilt by Andre Chapelon, then Chief Engineer of the P. O., to give effect to his ideas on improved thermal efficiency. No basic dimensions were changed, but the superheater was very much enlarged, the steam pipes and passages redesigned to present the freest possible steam flow, together with a double chimney; an ACFI feedwater heater was installed (visible behind the chimney and on the running plate), and poppet valves replaced piston valves. Finally, new bogie tenders were fitted in place of the old six-wheelers. In exchange for an increase in weight from 93 to 103 tons, maximum power output at the cylinders was increased from 2,100 to 3,500 h.p., with greater economy in fuel. Twenty-eight of the rebuilt engines were sold to the Nord, where some of them remained in service until 1966: one is to be preserved.

LONDON & NORTH EASTERN RAILWAY: A4 CLASS 4-6-2 (1935)

The London & North Eastern company, observing the feats of the Germans and Americans with lightweight highspeed trains, decided to run a streamliner themselves. There was some argument in favour of using a diesel railcar set, but a locomotive-hauled train was wisely preferred as more flexible and not tied to a fixed formation. H. N. Gresley designed the locomotive: a slightly enlarged but considerably improved version of his A3 Pacific of 1928 in a streamlined casing whose shape was determined after wind-tunnel tests. The A4s had three cylinders, 6' 8" wheels, and weighed 103 tons. The first was turned out by the Doncaster works in 1935: 35 more were built by 1938. The class was extremely successful: no. 4468 "Mallard", in 1938 with a 240-ton train achieved 126 m.p.h., a world record for steam traction, and during the war A4s also proved capable of working expresses weighing over 800 tons. The class was notably economical, too, especially after all of them had been fitted with double chimneys. All the A4s remained in service, working express passenger trains, until 1962, and the last was withdrawn in 1966. However, several have been preserved.

GERMAN STATE RAILWAYS: 05 CLASS 4-6-4 (1935)

During the early 1930s the German railways had caused a considerable stir with their high-speed light diesel railcars, of which the "Flying Hamburger" was the most famous. But although fast, these were inflexible and had limited accommodation; they proved the market, but now what was wanted was a locomotive capable of working a complete train at 100-m.p.h. speeds. In 1935 Borsig of Berlin built three such; streamlined 3-cylinder 4-6-4s, with 7' 7" driving wheels. Two were as illustrated right; the third, 05.003, was designed to burn pulverised coal and was turned about to run cab-first, with the tender at the chimney end. In May, 1936, on a test run with a 197-ton train 05.002 reached a speed of 124.6 m.p.h. on a nearly level track; only about 25% of the effort needed for this acceleration was due to gravity, compared with some 50% on Mallard's run two years later, so in that respect the 05's achievement was the more impressive. After 1944 all three engines were destreamlined, and 05.003 was rebuilt to conform closely with the others, as shown.

97

NEW YORK CENTRAL RAILROAD:
J3A CLASS 4-6-4 (1937)

For fast, heavy passenger service the limitation of a Pacific on a reasonably easily graded main line is in firebox capacity: six coupled wheels can provide the low-speed effort needed, but the horsepower demanded by sustained fast running means a big fire, and there comes a point where a four-wheeled trailing truck is needed to support it. (On a heavily-graded line or in freight service the need for more adhesive weight will be felt sooner: hence the 4-8-2 and 4-8-4). The New York Central introduced its first 4-6-4s (called "Hudsons" in American usage) in 1927, and they stayed in charge of their principal passenger trains until the last few years of steam. Class J3 was introduced in 1937, and two members of it, as shown here, were streamlined in 1941 to work the "Empire State Express", then newly equipped with stainless steel coaches.

UNION PACIFIC RAILROAD:
800 CLASS 4-8-4 (1937)

The UP's 800s were primarily intended for their transcontinental passenger trains, but were designed also with a view to fast freight service, and in practice they were used on both. The first 20 were built by the American Locomotive Co. in 1937, and 25 more followed between 1939 and 1944. Later engines in the series had double chimneys, whose virtues were little recognised in the USA: most companies were content to let their hard-worked single-chimney machines bellow impressively away without doing anything about the consequent inefficiency and waste of power at the front end. The 800s had 6' 5" driving wheels and weighed 225 tons; they were the second largest 4-8-4s ever built. After 1945 they were converted to burn oil. No. 844, the last of the class, has been retained in the UP's operating stock to work special trains.

SOUTH AFRICAN RAILWAYS:
23 CLASS 4-8-2 (1938)

In South Africa the greater proportion of traffic on non-electrified lines is still handled by steam power; and by some very fine locomotives too, many of which compare well for size with those of any other country in spite of running on the 3' 6" gauge. The largest of all are some of the numerous Garratts, but certain of the non-articulated locomotives run them close. One example is the 23 class, mixed traffic engines weighing 111 tons and with 5' 3" driving wheels, 136 of which were built by Henschel of Kassel and the Berliner Maschinenbau in 1938-9. Here No. 2552 is shown as she stood on first steam trial at her builders', not yet finished in her final coat of work-a-day black.

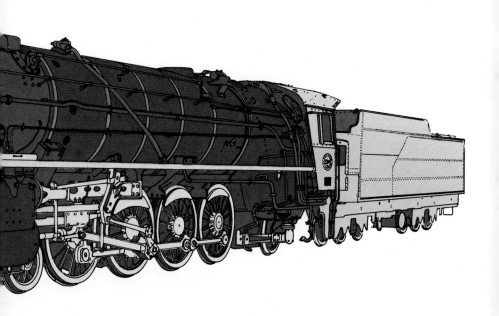

SPANISH NATIONAL RAILWAYS:
3100 CLASS 2-10-2 (1943)

Spanish railways were wrecked during the Civil War and slow to recover, partly because the larger war started in 1939 just as the smaller ended. Things were made worse by the fact that the system and especially its track had been decrepit before. These machines were the first really large modern engines to run in Spain, and dramatised the start of the recovery: 3-cylinder 2-10-2s with a 21-ton axleload and 57 square feet of grate, they were the most powerful of their kind in Europe. Twenty-two were built, followed in 1944 by some very similar heavy passenger 4-8-2s with two cylinders, bigger driving wheels, but the same boiler. The two classes are now arguably the most impressive examples of big steam power still working in Europe.

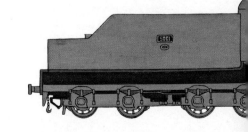

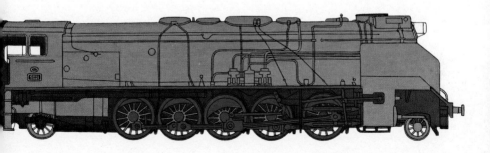

FRENCH NATIONAL RAILWAYS: 141R CLASS 2-8-2 (1945)

Devastated by war, the French railways in 1945 needed urgently many new locomotives to replace those which had been destroyed. There was no time for anything complex or tailormade; instead, one Canadian and three American builders between them mass-produced over 1,300 of these simple, rugged and conventional medium-sized mixed traffic 2-8-2s, marking the barest minimum of concessions to Gallic practice, consisting almost exclusively in the provision of rakish smoke deflectors. Rough and crude beside the sophisticated natives, the 141Rs nevertheless did extremely well in both freight and passenger service, despite a restriction to 67 m.p.h. imposed on them, and in the later days of steam the SNCF came to see their virtues. They burnt considerably more fuel than the compounds they worked alongside, but they were simpler to maintain.

UNITED STATES ARMY: STANDARD 0-6-0T (1942)

Not all American locomotives of the mid-twentieth century were giants: there remained a need for small machines for duties where a bigger engine would be wasted, or might even be unable to run, especially in industrial work. This design, intended for war service, is a typical example of the robust and extremely simple kind of machine that the Americans preferred for this work. Hundreds of these engines, all built to the British loading gauge, came to Europe after 1943 and settled down after the war in several countries, including Britain, France, Greece and Yugoslavia, where many of them are still at work.

109

UNION PACIFIC RAILROAD:
4000 CLASS 4-8-8-4 (1941)

These were the biggest steam locomotives ever built. Ready for the road, they weighed 340 tons—or about 40% less than the five diesels needed to equal their haulage capacity. They became famous as "Big Boys", because that was the name somebody chalked on the first one as it was being assembled in the American Locomotive Co. erecting shops. They were intended primarily for freight work in mountain country, but good design made them capable of speeds of 80 m.p.h. so that they could and did work passenger trains also, and ranged more widely, although their home ground was between Cheyenne and Salt Lake. They were coal-burners, fitted with mechanical stokers, as it was well beyond the capacity of any man to shovel coal fast enough to fire the 150 square feet of grate when the cylinders were putting out something over 9,000 h.p. Like most big American articulateds, they were not true Mallets, since all four cylinders used high pressure steam. The Big Boys lasted right up until final dieselisation in 1959; their owners were and still are proud of them, and several are preserved in various parts of the country.

110

111

EAST AFRICAN RAILWAYS:
59TH CLASS 4-8-2+2-8-4 (1955)

These are the most powerful metre-gauge locomotives ever built, and following the demise of American steam they became the most powerful steam engines in service in the world. Thirty-four of them were built by Beyer, Peacock of Manchester, the firm who held the Garratt patent, in 1955-6; ready for the road, they weigh 252 tons. More recently, they have been fitted with Geisl ejectors, which have enabled them to handle heavier trains on accelerated schedules over long mountain grades. Under local conditions, they are proving cheaper to operate than diesels.

The Garratt design was patented around the turn of the century by the Australian H. W. Garratt, working in conjunction with Beyer, Peacock. The object of the design, as with the Mallet, was to get the power of two locomotives out of one while retaining flexibility on curves. The advantage of the Garratt was that the boiler could be as large as necessary without infringing the loading gauge, and without becoming inefficiently lengthy. Garratts became common in most parts of central and southern Africa, and worked also in Australia and parts of Asia and South

America; in Europe they were rare, and in North America non-existent. But on those few lines where they did work alongside Mallets, they usually proved more successful.

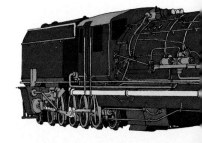

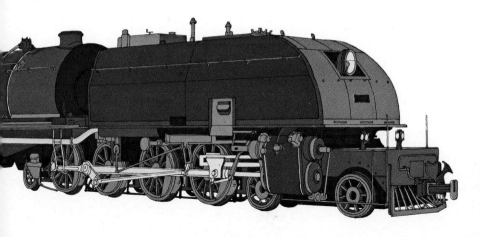

BRITISH RAILWAYS: 9F CLASS 2-10-0 (1954)

It would not be quite true to say that this was the only really adequate British freight locomotive, but it was certainly the only one built in quantity. And although it was long in coming, it was certainly one of the best designs ever in service in Britain. Simple, cheap, and robust, its moderate axleloading gave it a wide route availability: its relatively small driving wheels (5' diameter) proved no handicap to fast running, due to an excellent front end, and speeds of over 90 m.p.h. were reached in passenger service. The 9F was at home hauling heavy freights up hills, and (an important requirement in Britain) its brakes were able to hold them going down the other side. 251 were built between 1954 and 1960; they were the last steam locomotives built for British Railways.

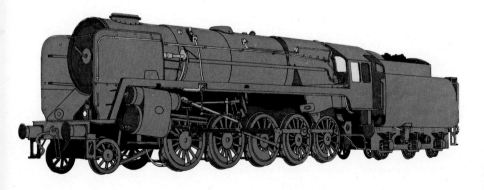

EAST GERMAN RAILWAYS:
01.5 CLASS 4-6-2 (1962)

The original German 01 class two-cylinder heavy Pacific was introduced in 1925; large numbers of them are still at work, and also of their bigger 3-cylinder successors of 1938, the 01.10s. In divided post-1945 Germany, the separate railway administrations faced the eventual necessity to rejuvenate the ageing 01s; in the West, some were straightforwardly rebuilt with a larger all-welded boiler, but in the East a more thorough reconstruction incorporated some of the new features developed since construction of new steam locomotives ceased. Along with a certain amount of exterior styling, new "Boxpok" driving wheels were used, and a Giesl Ejector, whose characteristic oblong chimney is visible. Production of 01.5s is still continuing; they seem likely to be the last new steam locomotives development to be undertaken in Europe.

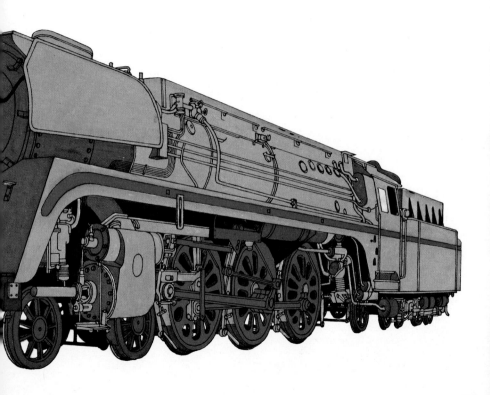

ITALIAN STATE RAILWAYS—E333 CLASS 1-C-1 ELECTRIC LOCO-MOTIVE (1922)

During the early years of railway electric development a number of problems had to be solved. One of these was the question of what kind of electricity to use; what voltage, and whether direct or alternating current, and if the latter, at what frequency. The advantage of direct current was that it could be used by a simple and compact motor, capable of starting under load and of fast running while giving full power over its whole speed range; this was exactly what was needed for locomotive work. On the other hand, only high-voltage alternating current could be transmitted over long distances, and expensive conversion equipment in substations was therefore needed for railways using D.C. In the early years A.C. traction motors were expensive, slow, and bulky, and so the simplicities of A.C. power supply were balanced by the need to use cumbersome locomotives, in which big, slow-running motors either drove the wheels through rods, as here, or drove D.C. dynamos feeding D.C. motors in turn—a method favoured in the USA, but leading to vast weight for comparatively low power output. This Italian example is unusual in that it ran on 3-phase A.C. (3,600 volts at $16\frac{2}{3}$ cycles); a variety of alternating current in which, instead of the two wires carrying current balancing each other at 180° phases with which we are familiar in the household and in most industrial use, three wires (two overhead plus earth return) carry current alternating at 120° phases to each other. This system had some advantages in ease of control and construction, but had the drawback that the locomotive could only run at two or three fixed speeds, uphill and downhill, without suffering from overheating and eventual failure in service. This system of electrification is not yet quite extinct; a little survives in Italy, and in Spain.

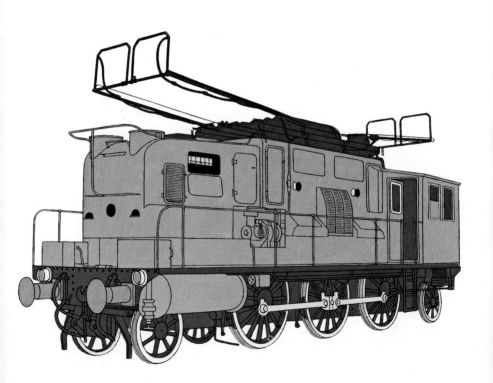

FRENCH NATIONAL RAILWAYS—CC7100 ELECTRIC LOCOMOTIVE (1953)

Until the mid-1950s, the standard French system of railway electrification used direct current at 1,500 volts, and most of the main lines south of Paris had been converted by this method before the SNCF developed the 25,000 volt 50-cycle A.C. system, using locomotives in which rectifiers converted the current to D.C. before it reached the traction motors. Once at a state where it was economically competitive, the high-voltage A.C. installation offered advantages in saving of first cost, so the more recently electrified lines in the north and east of the country use it; but the D.C. system, once installed, is as completely satisfactory as the new from the operational point of view.

The CC 7100 was the last major class of locomotives designed by the SNCF in a D.C. version only, and nowadays forms the mainstay of express services on the ex-P.L.M. main line from Paris to Lyons and Marseilles. With six motored axles, it weighs 107 tons, and is capable of developing slightly over 5,000 horsepower. No. CC 7107 shares with a slightly smaller four-axled machine, which reached the same speed the following day, the world rail speed record of 331 kilometres per hour (205.7 m.p.h.), achieved with a test train on the Bordeaux-Bayonne line on March 28th, 1955.

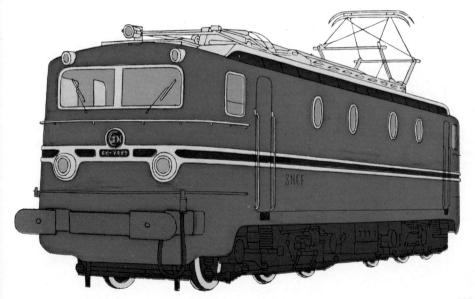

ELECTRO-MOTIVE COMPANY (CLEVELAND, OHIO): PETROL-ELECTRIC RAILCAR (1924)

The Electro-Motive Company were the first American firm to produce a series of reliable internal-combustion engined rail vehicles, though other companies had previously produced railcars and locomotives for commercial service on a small scale. The basis of the design was a petrol engine of the kind used for driving buses; later, petrol was replaced by kerosene, which was less inflammable and less heavily taxed. The first E.M. car was built in 1924, and during the next seven years over 400 were sold, increasing in size from 170 horsepower in the first to some which were capable of hauling trailers. This particular example, in service on the Pacific Great Eastern Railway in British Columbia, was one of the later ones with a 250 h.p. engine. Like all its sisters, it worked only in one direction.

Rural stopping passenger services have always been a headache to their owners; by no means easy to operate, and even harder to run at a profit, their motive power requirements were quite different from those of any other sort of train in that high speed was needed but only low horsepower. As road competition began to take toll of their local passengers, railways looked for the chance to save the cost of running steam engines on these light workings, so these "doodlebugs" found a ready market. But eventually trade dwindled further, services were abandoned, and few of them now remain. A modernised version of the same thing was developed in the late 1940s; the survivors of these are now generally on duties which would have needed a whole train twenty years ago. On the other hand, the Electro-Motive Company prospers; by 1930 it had built railcars so powerful that the engines occupied their entire body space, and they had therefore become locomotives. Acquired by the giant General Motors Company in that year, they went on to become the world's biggest manufacturers of diesel locomotives.

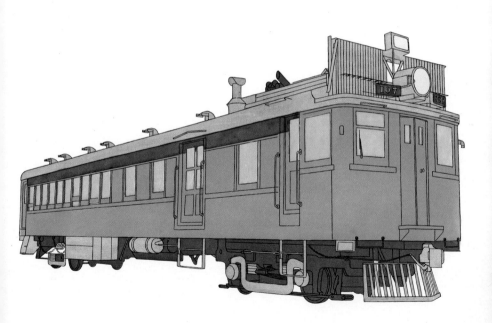

GERMAN FEDERAL RAILWAY: V200 CLASS DIESEL-HYDRAULIC (1954)

Diesel locomotives have had half a century of development; they were pioneered in Germany, but first widely adopted in the USA. The economics of the essentially very simple diesel motor have always been attractive: the problem was how to marry its power output, which exists at a rapidly-turning shaft, with the need to start a heavy, stationary train. The motor-car solves a similar problem by the unsound device of the clutch, which transmits power by friction in a manner abhorrent to sound engineering practice, and gets away with it due to its light weight; but with a heavy train this is not possible.

Since the electric motor shares with steam power the ability to start under load, the commonest answer is to use the diesel engine to drive a generator. This produces electricity which is fed to a number of traction motors driving the wheels. Although reliable and efficient, this chain of equipment is heavy and expensive, and several railways are backing the development of a lighter and cheaper alternative in the diesel-hydraulic locomotive. Here the transmission depends on a torque converter, where input and output shafts are coupled through the first driving, and the second being driven by, moving oil. Since this

works well only over a limited range of variation between input and output shaft speeds, it needs to be combined with a gearbox. But the overall effect is to make possible a locomotive which for equal power can weigh as little as half as much as a corresponding diesel-electric. The V.200 is a 2,000-horse-power machine weighing only 77 tons; it is unusual also in having inside bearings to its wheels. In other respects its layout conforms to standard modern European practice. Fast passenger trains form an important part of the work of European diesels, which are powerful enough to haul them without assistance; hence, although fitted for multiple-unit working, they normally run singly, and to save the need to turn at the end of each run, they have a cab at each end. Although it is possible to build a diesel having one more or less central cab with vision in either direction, generally the bulk of the machinery makes this difficult on a high-powered locomotive.

GENERAL ELECTRIC COMPANY:
U25C TYPE DIESEL-ELECTRIC (1963)

The first American main-line diesel loco-motives were streamlined and intended for high-speed passenger service at least as much as freight work. Since they were only moderately powerful (not more than 1,500 h.p.), several were needed to sub-stitute for one large steam locomotive, but since they could be remote-controlled only one crew were needed and two, three, four or more units thus in fact became one engine. In American practice diesels with cabs at each end are almost unknown, since with multiple-unit working it is possible to have a driving position at each end of the whole combination, which often includes cab-less "helper" units in the middle.

With the decline of passenger trains in the USA, the streamlined diesels of the first generation are dying out, and are being replaced by utilitarian machines of this kind. On the other hand, American loco-motive development has been much less adventurous with diesels than with steam, and mechanical features have changed only very slowly through the years. The traditional American diesel is very heavy by European standards, not very power-ful, and is driven by a big slow-running engine. On the other hand, this con-servatism does produce a machine whose reliability is not often equalled in Euro-pean practice. But due to the need to in-crease freight train speeds to compete with road transport, American power ratings are creeping up. General Electric's U25B of 1962 was the first US diesel to develop as much as 2,500 h.p.; apart from having 8 wheels it was identical with the U25C shown here.

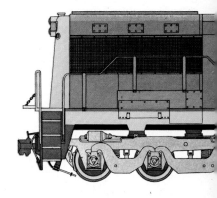

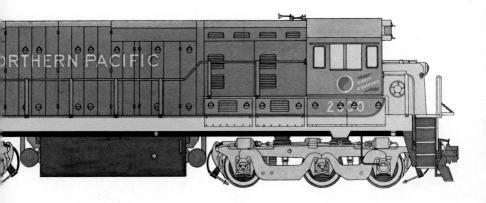

ACKNOWLEDGEMENTS
The author and publishers would like to
record their acknowledgements of the
assistance given towards the preparation
of this book, both in provision of pic-
torial material and of supporting inform-
ation, by Messrs. A. E. Durrant, and P. M.
Kalla-Bishop, together with "La Vie du
Rail" of Paris, the Kalmbach Publishing
Co. of Milwaukee, Wisconsin, and the
Association of American Railroads.